Christmas Greetings

To...

Published in Nashville, Tennessee,
by Thomas Nelson, Inc.

Project Developer: Lisa Stilwell
Designed by Susan Browne Design,
Nashville, TN

ISBN-10: 1–4041–0507–7
ISBN-13: 978–1–4041–0507–2

Printed and bound in China

www.thomasnelson.com

The images on these pages
are drawn from vintage
Christmas postcards circa
1880-1920 in the collection of
Lucinda Poole Cockrell.

Lucinda Cockrell

A Victorian Christmas

MANDOLIN by
Butch Baldassari

Published by
THOMAS NELSON™
Since 1798

www.thomasnelson.com

Christmas Rose

Christmas Rose this Christmas Morn,
Methinks I hear thee softly say
"In Bethlehem a Child was born
Who bled to take my thorn away!"
Hence musing thus through Earthly bowers
Oh, let us look from them to those
Where shines the King—The flower of flowers—
The great—the one-true CHRISTMAS ROSE!

By Francis Dave, from a Marcus Ward Christmas postcard,
ca.1884

A Bright and Happy Christmas Day

Little child with smiling eyes,
That look so innocent and wise,
'Twas such as those one Christmasday,
Who in a lowly manger lay—
And for the children still we make
High festival for His dear sake.

By Helen Marion Burnside,
from a Court Greeting Card,
1880–1899

A Happy Christmas

On all our days as they unfold,

Heaven pours its blessing down,

For all our days are grains of gold

From love's immortal crown!

And so a glad Christmas be thine;

God's blessing too, come shade or shine!

From a Christmas postcard, ca. 1885

Over the mountains,
and cities and dells,
Ring Christmas Peace and Joy
—Oh Bells!

From a Raphael Tuck & Sons card 1880s

A Happy Christmas

Christmas blessings
Fill thy heart,
May the sadness
All depart,
For thy Lord
Was born today.
Let Him wipe
Thy tears away.

From a Christmas postcard, ca.1885

No doubt you will have often heard
That 'times are very hard,'
But, spite of threatened poverty,
I've bought this little Card;
Like widow's mite, to show you that
My love has never ceas'd,
And make you have a thought for me,
Through Christmas' merry feast.

From a postcard, ca. 1900

When the ruby-eyed holly bush

    gladdens the sight,

And the pearls of the mistletoe

    sparkle with light,

Think of one whose fond heart with

    affection is beating,

Who now sends with love this new Postal Card greeting.

From a Christmas postcard, published by John S. Day, London, 1870

With Loving Wishes for a Happy Christmas

I know you wish me merry

All the season through

And so with all my heart, dear

Here's the same to you.

By Helen Marion Burnside from a Raphael Tuck card, 1890–1900

The wintry earth in white is clad,

The year draws near its end,

To give you greeting blithe and glad

   The old, old wish we send.

   Bring in the Yule log to the hall,

   And let the mirth ring clear;

  Here's Merry Christmas to you all!

A bright and happy Year!

From an original card by Ernest Nister, London,
printed in Bavaria, 1880–1890

He laughs in every glad heart's beating,
He links with firmer love the true.
O glad as bells his name repeating
May old King Christmas come to you.

From a card published by Eyre & Spottiswoode, 1890–1900

Each Christmas as it passes
Some change to us doth bring
Yet to our friends the closer,
As Time creeps on, we cling.

From a Victorian Christmas card, ca. 1900

On Christmas day the year
Doth all her jewels show,
The holly rubies red
And pearls of mistletoe.

From a Prang Christmas card, 1882

With the Season's Greetings
A Merry Christmas to you all
And merry hearts both great and small.

From an H. Rothe Christmas card, 1880

"...and it was always said of him, that he knew how to keep Christmas well, if any man alive possessed that knowledge. May that be truly said of us, and all of us!"

From Charles Dickens's *A Christmas Carol*, 1843

With the ivy dark and the glorious laurel,
Say, where is the critic would like to quarrel,
Crowned, as they are, with sharp spears of holly?
And what is more charming than Christmas folly?
Only shew me the man, who at Christmas time
Will not swallow nonsense if put into rhyme.
    So rime—rime,
    Christmas time;
    Let holly
    Crown folly,
And make us all jolly.

By Thomas Crofton Croker, from *Recollections of Old Christmas*, a masque originally performed on Christmas Eve in 1850 by the "aristocratic inhabitants of Grimston Hall in Yorkshire," featuring such characters as Mince-Pie and Baron of Beef

Christmas, all hail!—without though wild the storm,

Within, good fires, good fare, shall keep us warm;

And the huge log, in chimney blazing bright,

Make joyous sparkle through the merry night;

While pleasant tales are told around the hearth,

Where mingle pious thoughts with thoughts of earth.

By Thomas Crofton Croker, from *Recollections of Old Christmas*, 1850

Peace and goodwill—forgetfulness of wrong,
Are attributes to Christmas that belong.
Heap high the fire, and make us royal crown,
It is our pleasure here to sit us down.
Who cares how deeply now the snow-flakes fall?
Let rosemary and bays bedeck the wall.

By Thomas Crofton Croker, from *Recollections of Old Christmas*, 1850

A Christmas Croak

Oh, rest you, merry gentlemen!

Let nothing you dismay;

But be prepared to meet the woes

That come with Christmas Day.

Look out! look out! your winter clothes,

To face the season's ills;

And muster cash and fortitude

To meet your Christmas bills.

And 'tis tidings of comfort and joy.

By Robert B. Brough, from *A Cracker Bon-Bon for Christmas Parties: Consisting of Christmas Pieces, for Private Representation, and Other Seasonable Matter, in Prose and Verse,* 1852.

The Approach of Christmas

The time draws near the birth of Christ,
The moon is hid, the night is still;
A single church below the hill
Is pealing, folded in the mist

A single peal of bells below
That wakens at this hour of rest
A single murmur in the breast,
That these are not the bells I know

Like strangers' voices here they sound,
In lands where not a memory strays,
Nor landmark breathes of other days.
But all is new unhallow'd ground.

From Tennyson's "In Memoriam," *Harper's New Monthly* magazine / Volume 1, Issue 4, September 1850

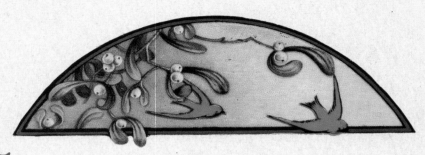

Time was, with most of us, when Christmas-day encircling all our limited world like a magic ring, left nothing out for us to miss or seek; bound together all our home enjoyments, affections, and hopes; grouped every thing and every one around the Christmas fire; and made the little picture shining in our bright young eyes, complete.

"Therefore, as we grow older, let us be more thankful that the circle of our Christmas associations and of the lessons that they bring, expands! Let us welcome every one of them, and summon them to take their places by the Christmas hearth.

"Welcome, every thing! Welcome, alike what has been, and what never was, and what we hope may be, to your shelter underneath the holly, to your places round the Christmas fire, where what is sits open-hearted!"

From *What Christmas Is, As We Grow Older*, by Charles Dickens,
from *Harper's New Monthly* magazine / Volume 4, Issue 21, February 1852

A Happy Christmas and a Bright New Year

Sunny skies and fragrant flowers

Fill with joy these Christmas hours.

Bless today and stay with you,

All the coming bright year

through.

From a Raphael Tuck postcard, ca. 1900

Our Christmas-Tree

My tree is very high,
In fact reaches to the sky,
And sweet birds passing by
There fold their wings.

Its leaves are very green,
With a wondrous glossy sheen,
And the summer wind serene
Around it sings.

And I've hung upon my tree
A myriad gifts you see,
And all the world is free
To come and take.

There is love and gentle mirth,
There's a happy home and hearth,
And "Peace to all on Earth,"
For the Christ-child's sake.

There are sweet and soothing words
Melodious as the birds,
There is charity that herds
With the poor forlorn.

There are pardons for all wrongs,
And cheerful peasant songs,
And the virtue that belongs
To the country home.

For Heaven has blessed the shoots,
And Fancy riped the fruits,
And my heart is round the roots
Of our Christmas-tree.

By Fitz-James O'Brien, from *Harper's New Monthly* magazine / Volume 20, Issue 118, March 1860

Christmas at Trinity

Sweet bells of hope! I heard you, with a spirit stronger growing,
While over me eternal stars with love and strength were glowing;
And when the Christmas noon-tide came, and came the gilded thronging,
I could look on all the happiness nor feel the lonesome longing;
While on children lightly leaping, while on maid and lover blushing,
While on mothers proud and comely, on the living river rushing,
Down showered tumultuous music from the belfry of Old Trinity—
Merry chiming for His birth, and grave songs for His Divinity!

From *Harper's New Monthly* magazine / Volume 30, Issue 177, February 1865

At Christmas Time

TONIGHT WE GATHER ROUND THE HEARTH
WHILE NOW THE CHRISTMAS TIME IS NEAR,
THE TIME WE KEEP WITH SONG AND MIRTH,
WITH NOISY GAMES AND FESTAL CHEER.

RING BELLS OF CHEER, RING IN THE DAY
WHEN CRUEL WRONG AT LAST SHALL CEASE;
WHEN FEUD AND HATE SHALL PASS AWAY,
AND BRING THE REIGN OF LOVE AND PEACE!

From *Harper's New Monthly* magazine / Volume 32, Issue 187, December 1865

Christmas Carol

When the Holy Babe was born,
Angels, singing, woke the morn,
Chanting praises to our Lord,
Peace on earth and sweet accord;
For He came to set us free;
He was born our Lord to be;
From sin and pain to set us free.

From *Harper's New Monthly magazine* / Volume 46,
Issue 272, January 1873.

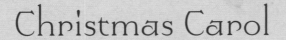

A Jolly Christmas

Just a little spray of holly,
Neatly tied with ribbon, gay,
Sent to make your heart right jolly
On this gladsome
Christmas Day.

From a postcard, ca. 1900

The Legend of the Mistletoe

His reindeer team shook their sliver bells,

And sniffed the north wind gladly;

"Now," Santa Claus cried, "hurrah for a ride!

These earth folks need me sadly."

They skimmed the frozen polar sea, like dart from cross-bow springing;

O'er snow-clad plains they swiftly sped, like swallows southward winging;

Through forests dim, where ice-clad trees in ghostly garb were bending;

Through wizard realms, where night and day in light and shade were blending.

Like flitting dream sped the reindeer team,

The Saint cheering "Onward!" loudly.

From *Harper's New Monthly* magazine /
Volume 44, Issue 260, January 1872

A Christmas Thought

Lo! in the woods, beneath the frost-kissed hill,
The holly lights the path—December's rose—
And underneath the scarlet berry grows,
As if to tell us Love is living still:

Living, albeit under ruder skies;
Though the glad glory of the year be past,
With frost and death Love lingers to the last,
And in Love's breast her blossom never dies.

'Tis nursed with thoughts that come with Christmas chime
That "gracious time" when Love and Peace are crowned,
When the world's woes in one great joy are drowned:
The summer of the soul is Christmas-time.

From *Harper's New Monthly* magazine / Volume 66, Issue 392, January 1883

A Joyful Christmas

Fair be your days that come and go,

I write these lines to let you know

That greetings fond and wishes true

Dear heart, all these I wish to you.

From a postcard, "Of Good Cheer," ca. 1900

29

Christmas

This is the Christmas sentiment of to-day, as it was of Shakespeare's time. It is the most human and kindly of seasons, as fully penetrated and irradiated with the feeling of human brotherhood, which is the essential spirit of Christianity, as the month of June with sunshine and the balmy breath of roses. Santa Claus coming down the chimney loaded with gifts is but the symbol of the gracious influence which at this time descends from heaven into every heart. The day dawns with a benediction; it passes in holiday happiness; and ends in soft and pensive regret. It could not be the most beautiful of festivals if it were doctrinal, or dogmatic, or theological, or local. It is a universal holiday because it is the jubilee of a universal sentiment, moulded only by a new epoch, and subtly adapted to newer forms of the old faith.

The day that commemorates His birth is the festival of humanity, as the inspiring sentiment of actual life. The lovely legends of the day, the stories, and the songs, and the half fairy-lore that gathers around it, the ancient traditions of dusky woods and mystic rites; the magnificence or simplicity of Christian observance . . . the lighting of Christmas trees and hanging up of Christmas stockings, the profuse giving, the happy family meetings, the dinner, the game, the dance—they are all the natural signs and symbols, the flower and fruit, of Christmas. For Christmas is the day of days which declares the universal human consciousness that peace on earth comes only from good-will to man.

From *Harper's New Monthly* magazine / Volume 68, Issue 403, December 1883

A Christmas Card

I have no purse of gold, my dear,
With which to buy you dainty things;
The purse is empty, and the gold
Has flown away as if on wings;
So, sweetest wife in all the world,
Tho' you possess the greater part,
I'll give to you on Christmas day
Another fraction of my heart.

By K. D. W., from *Harper's New Monthly* magazine / Volume 86, Issue 511, December 1892

The Poor Lover's Christmas Card

I haven't much to send this day,
    No jewel rare, no volume fine;
But if you will, why then you may
    Share with me this right hand of mine.

And who knows but that it may hap
    This hand, to-day so void of thrift,
May yet pour fortunes in the lap
    Of her who takes it as a gift?

From *Harper's New Monthly* magazine / Volume 90, Issue 535, December 1894

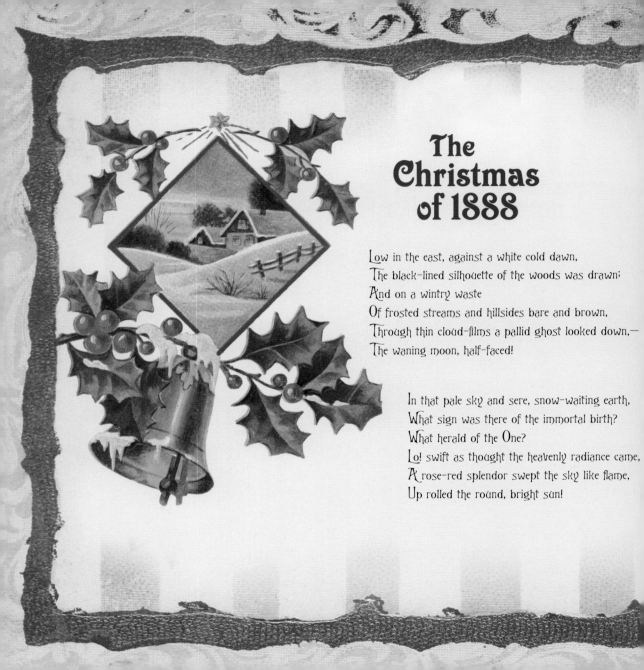

The Christmas of 1888

Low in the east, against a white cold dawn,
The black-lined silhouette of the woods was drawn;
And on a wintry waste
Of frosted streams and hillsides bare and brown,
Through thin cloud-films a pallid ghost looked down,—
The waning moon, half-faced!

In that pale sky and sere, snow-waiting earth,
What sign was there of the immortal birth?
What herald of the One?
Lo! swift as thought the heavenly radiance came,
A rose-red splendor swept the sky like flame,
Up rolled the round, bright sun!

And all was changed. From a transfigured world
The moon's ghost fled, the smoke of home-hearths curled
Up the still air unblown.
In Orient warmth and brightness, did that morn
O'er Nain and Nazareth, when the Christ was born,
Break fairer than our own?

The morning's promise noon and eve fulfilled
In warm, soft sky and landscape hazy-hilled
And sunset fair as they:
A sweet reminder of His holiest time,
A summer-miracle in our winter clime,
God gave a perfect day.
The near was blended with the old and far,
And Bethlehem's hillside and the Magi's star
Seemed here, as there and then:
Our homestead pine tree was the Syrian palm,
Our heart's desire the angels' midnight psalm,
Peace and good-will to men!

By John Greenleaf Whittier, from
The Atlantic Monthly / Volume 63,
Issue 377, March 1889

The Christ of the Snows:
A Norwegian Legend

For surely He cometh,
Now midnight is near;
The wild winds, like wolf packs,
Have fled in their fear,

Or hid in far fjords,
Or died on the floes:
For surely He cometh,
Our Christ of the Snows.

Sing Christmas, sweet Christmas,
All good men below;
Sing Christmas that bringeth
Our Christ of the Snow.

By S. Weir Mitchell, from *The Atlantic Monthly /
Volume 55, Issue 327, January 1885*

Christmas Greetings

Just a line on a card to say
   I am thinking of you today
Just a line on a card, but Oh
   What a world of meaning can go
In simple words, when the writer is I
   And you are the one to whom the words fly.

From a postcard, 1914

A Christmas Question

It was after the maze and the mirth of the dance,
  Where a spray of green mistletoe swayed,
That I met—and I vow that the meeting was chance!—
  With a very adorable maid.

I stood for a moment in tremor of doubt,
  Then kissed her, half looking for war;
But—"Why did you wait, sir?" she said, with a pout.
  "Pray, what is the mistletoe for?"

By Clinton Scollard, from *The Century*, a popular quarterly /
Volume 51, Issue 2, December 1895

Songs of Christmas: Christmas Eve

A legend tells us that on Christmas Eve the Christ-child, after visiting mortals, goes to Fairy-land, and there stays till morning light. If any of the fairy folk choose to follow him, he takes them with him; they are born on earth as human beings, and if faithful are saved.

"Hasten, brothers, hasten!
Ringing sweet and clear,
Fairy bells are chiming,
Christmas Eve is near!
Then the dear Child Jesus,
All in robes of white,
Dances with us gaily
Till the morning light!"

Three Christmas Chimes

Sing your joy, O Christmas chime!
Let us keep the Christmas-time
Let all strife and hatred cease,
Kindness live, good-will and peace.
Thus we keep the Christmas-time.

Sing your joy, O Christmas chime!
Let us keep the Christmas-time
Love shall be the law to bind
In one band all humankind.
Thus we keep the Christmas-time.

By Constantina E. Brooks, from *The Century*, a popular quarterly / Volume 39, Issue 2, December 1889

Hymn for Christmas Eve

But Christmas cheer to-night is near,
And Christmas thoughts are high and holy.
We weep no tears for dying years;
Be theirs of life the common story;
But give to truth eternal youth,
And crown its natal day with glory.

The hearth is warm, though fierce with storm
The bitter wind without be blowing;
For Christmas time's the tropic clime
Of hearts with cheerful homage glowing.
The winter grieves o'er withered leaves,
And leafless branches sigh and quiver;
But green shall be our Christmas tree,
And beautiful, in faith, forever.

By A. M. Ide Jr., from *The Living Age* / Volume 52, Issue 661, January 24, 1857

The Pauper's Christmas Carol

Christmas comes but once a year.

Bright and blessed is the time,

Sorrows end and joys begin,

While the bells with merry chime

Ring the Day of Plenty in!

But the happy tide to hail

With a sigh or with a tear,

Heigh ho!

I hardly know—

Christmas comes but once a year!

From *The Living Age* / Volume 1, Issue 3, June 1, 1844

MISTLETOE

Sitting under the mistletoe
(Pale-green, fairy mistletoe),
One last candle burning low,
All the sleepy dancers gone,
Just one candle burning on,
Shadows lurking everywhere:
Someone came, and kissed me there.

Tired I was; my head would go
Nodding under the mistletoe
(Pale-green, fairy mistletoe),
No footsteps came, no voice, but only,
Just as I sat there, sleepy, lonely,
Stooped in the still and shadowy air
Lips unseen—and kissed me there.

By Walter de la Mare, 1913

Slowly Fall the Snow-Flakes

Slowly fall the snow-flakes,

Clothing earth in white,

Sweetly bells are chiming,

On this Christmas night

Dark the earth aforetime,

White on Christmas morn;

Christ the curse reversing,

Mary's Son is born.

A Christmas song by W. Borrow, from *Carols Old and New: For Use at Christmas and Other Seasons of the Christian Year* by Charles L. Hutchins, 1916

Everywhere, Everywhere, Christmas To-Night

Christmas in lands of the fir tree and pine,
Christmas in lands of the palm tree and vine;
Christmas where snow-peaks stand solemn and white,
Christmas where cornfields lie sunny and bright;
Everywhere, everywhere, Christmas to-night!

From *Carols Old and New: For Use at Christmas and Other Seasons of the Christian Year*
by Charles L. Hutchins, 1916

Christmas Songs Are Ringing Now

Christmas songs are ringing now,

Thro' the wintry sky,

Christmas strains by children sung

Swell the song on high,

For one is born, the Prince of Peace,

Whose reign shall never, never cease.

Our hearts are light,

Our hopes are bright,

At Thy coming, O Prince of Peace,

And we of Thy fold, like children of old,

Sing Hosanna, O Prince of Peace.

By Knapp, from Carols Old and New: For Use at
Christmas and Other Seasons of the Christian Year
by Charles L. Hutchins, 1916

All Children Are on Christmas Eve

All children are on Christmas Eve
As busy as can be;
They hang their little stockings up
For Santa Claus to see.
How very careful they must be
To have them stout and strong;
For Santa Claus has many a toy,
To please this merry throng.
Hush! Hark! I hear the tiny reindeer
Come pattering on the snow;
Now quickly get you into bed,
Or else away they'll go.

From *Carols Old and New: For Use at Christmas and Other Seasons of the Christian Year* by Charles L. Hutchins, 1916

Good Night

Good night, dear little dreamers,
　　May visions fair and bright
Of Santa Claus and Christmas
　　Bring joy to you this night;
May angels guard your slumbers
　　Till the dawn of light.

From *Carols Old and New: For Use at Christmas and Other Seasons of the Christian Year* by Charles L. Hutchins, 1916

49

Let Music Break on This Blest Morn

Let music break on this blest morn,
And sweetly echo back to heav'n,
For lo! The promis'd Son is born,
The long expected One is giv'n.

From *Carols Old and New: For Use at Christmas and Other Seasons of the Christian Year*
by Charles L. Hutchins, 1916

O'er Hill and Dell the Christmas Bell

O'er hill and dell the Christmas bell
Is ringing far and wide;
Let all rejoice,
With cheerful voice,
And peace on earth abide.
For Christ is born
This happy morn,
Hark! Hark! The Angels sing;
Good-will and love,
From Heav'n above,
To all mankind they bring.

By Henry Knight, from Carols Old
and New For Use at Christmas and
Other Seasons of the Christian
Year by Charles L. Hutchins, 1916

Christmas Time Has Come Again

Christmas time has come again,
Time to us so dear;
It will bring to all the world
Gladness and good cheer.

Ring on, bells! Ring on, bells!
Ring on, Christmas bells!
Joy and Peace to all mankind,
Ring out, merry bells!

By Charles L. Hutchins, 1900, from *Carols Old and New: For Use at Christmas and Other Seasons of the Christian Year* by Charles L. Hutchins, 1916

A Christmas Carol

So now is come our joyful feast,
Let every man be jolly;
Each room with ivy leaves is dressed,
And every post with holly.

Then wherefore in these merry days
Should we, I pray, be duller?
No, let us sing some roundelays
To make our mirth the fuller.

And whilst we thus inspired sing,
Let all the streets with echoes ring;
Woods, and hills, and everything
Bear witness we are merry.

By George Wither 1588–1667

A Christmas Carol

I HEAR ALONG OUR STREET
PASS THE MINSTREL THRONGS;
HARK! THEY PLAY SO SWEET,
ON THEIR HAUTBOYS, CHRISTMAS SONGS!
LET US BY THE FIRE
EVER HIGHER
SING THEM TILL THE NIGHT EXPIRE!

From the *Noel Bourguignon De Gui Barozai*. By Henry Wadsworth Longfellow, From *Longfellow's Poetical Works*, 1893, published by Henry Frowde, London *[a hautboy is an oboe]*

It is well to be merry and wise, as well as to be thoughtful and sad, when the old year is dying. And if we have no other reason to be mindful of the coming of the end, there is enough to make us think of it in the settlement of our accounts, which must be attended to about these days.

"Oh! The bills, Christmas bills!
What a world of misery
Their memory instills!
As the merchants with their quills
Stuck behind their 'ears polite,'
So caressingly invite
Your kind and prompt attention
To their bills!
How they dun, dun, dun,
As they kindly urge upon
Your earnest attention their blessed little bills,
Little bills!"

From *Harper's New Monthly* magazine / Volume 12, Issue 67, December 1855

I know I wished you this before
But every year I wish it more:
"A Merry Christmas."

From a postcard, 1916

A Merry Christmas

The Christmas card looks so tiny, I know,
But be sure somewhere about it
Is a wish so gay
For your gladness to-day
That you wouldn't be without it.

From a postcard, ca. 1900

A Joyful Christmas

May all your days be happy days,
But added blessings fall
Upon to-day, that it may be
The brightest of them all.

From a postcard, 1914

A Merry Christmas to You

A Happy New Year,
Health and prosperity,
Your life to cheer,
With every blessing,
For the bright New Year.

From a Christmas/New Year's greeting card, late nineteenth century

A Merry Christmas.

This Card to wish You Happiness & Prosperity.

Every Christmas greeting is another link in the chain of our friendship, which each year grows stronger and longer until, someday, it will reach from Earth to Heaven.

From a postcard, 1913

Christmas Day

(Uncle Seth loquitur)

By Alice Williams Brotherton, from
The Century, a popular quarterly /
Volume 43, Issue 2, December 1891

[*Res ispa loquitar* is a legal term
from the Latin meaning literally,
"The thing itself speaks" but is
more often translated "The thing
speaks for itself".]

A good old-fashioned Chris'mas, with the logs upon the hearth,
The table filled with feasters, an' the room a-roar 'ith mirth,
With the stockin's crammed to bu'stin', an' the medders piled 'ith snow—
A good old-fashioned Chris'mas like we had so long ago!

Now that's the thing I'd like to see ag'in afore I die,
But Chris'mas in the city here it's different, oh my!
With the crowded hustle-bustle of the slushy, noisy street,
An' the scowl upon the faces of the strangers that you meet.

Oh, there's buyin', plenty of it, of a lot o' gorgeous toys;
An' it takes a mint o' money to please modern girls and boys.
Why, I mind the time a jack-knife an' a toffy-lump for me
Made my little heart an' stockin' jus' chock-full o' Chris'mas glee.

An' there's feastin'. Think o' feedin' with these stuck-up city folk!
Why, ye have to speak in whispers, an' ye dar'sn't crack a joke.
Then remember how the tables looked all crowded with your kin,
When you couldn't hear a whistle blow across the merry din!

You see I'm so old-fashioned-like I don't care much for style,
An' to eat your Chris'mas banquets here I wouldn't go a mile;
I'd rather have, like Solomon, a good yarb-dinner set
With real old friends than turkle soup with all the nobs you'd get.

There's my next-door neighbor Gurley—fancy how his brows 'u'd lift
If I'd holler, "Merry Chris'mas! Caught, old fellow, Chris'mas gift!"
Lordy-Lord, I'd like to try it! Guess he'd nearly have a fit.
Hang this city stiffness, anyways, I can't get used to it.

Then your heart it kept a-swellin' till it nearly bu'st your side,
An' by night your jaws were achin' with your smile four inches wide,
An your enemy, the wo'st one, you'd just grab his hand, an' say:
"Mebbe both of us was wrong, John. Come, let's shake. It's Chris'mas Day!"

Mighty little Chris'mas spirit seems to dwell 'tween city walls,
Where each snowflake brings a soot-flake for a brother as it falls;
Mighty little Chris'mas spirit! An' I'm pinin', don't you know,
For a good old-fashioned Chris'mas like we had so long ago.

A Victorian Christmas

1. God Rest Ye Merry Gentlemen/ We Three Kings
2. Do You Hear What I Hear?
3. What Child Is This?
4. Angels We Have Heard on High
5. The Little Drummer Boy
6. Beautiful Star of Bethlehem
7. Joy to the World
8. Silent Night
9. It Came Upon a Midnight Clear
10. O Little Town of Bethlehem
11. Away in a Manger
12. O Holy Night
13. The First Noel
14. Deck the Halls
15. We Wish You a Merry Christmas

Musicians

BUTCH BALDASSARI - mandolins, mandola, octave mandolin, nylon string guitar
SAM BACCO - percussion
MIKE BUB - string bass
SHAWN CAMP - fiddle
JOHN CATCHINGS - cello
MARK HORWITZ - flute
RANDY HOWARD - fiddle, guitars
MARK SCHATZ - string bass
TIM STAFFORD - guitar
GENE WOOTEN - dobro
ANDREA ZONN - viola

Produced by Butch Baldassari
Recorded by Rich Alder at STUDIO 2000, Nashville, TN
Mixed by Rocky Schnaars at Recording Arts, Nashville, TN
Mastered by John Eberle at Americana Mastering, Nashville, TN
All arrangements published by Slocum Hollow Songs BMI, except "The Little Drummer Boy", "Do You Hear What I Hear", and "Beautiful Star of Bethlehem"